Plant Life

Contents

Revision

Did you know . . ?

★ **There are different kinds of plants but they have things in common.**

★ **Plants need certain things to stay alive and to grow.**

Plants come in many different shapes and sizes.
These are all flowering plants.

These plants do not have flowers.

Almost all plants have green leaves at some time in the year.

All plants grow.

Task 1

What do other people say about plants?

Sometimes when people think of plants, they only think of small flowering plants.

 Carry out a survey. Ask five people – adults or children – to name five different plants.

Write down what they say.
What type of plants do people usually think about?

PCM 1

Look at the different groups of plants on Photocopy Master 1.
Fill in the tables on the Photocopy Master.

Write the answers to these questions.

- Which type of plant did people name most?
- Were there any types of plant that were not named at all?
- Why do you think you got these results?

Plants have things in common.
Here are two types of flowering plants. They both have roots, a stem, leaves and flowers.

Horse chestnut

Flowers
You will find out more about flowers in this book.

Leaves
You will find out more about leaves in this book.

Stem
Plants use their stems to carry things they need, like water and food, to other parts of the plant.

Roots
Plants use roots to take in water and small amounts of other things from the soil. Plants also use roots to anchor themselves in the ground.

Dandelion

Remember . . .

Plants need certain things to stay alive and to grow.

Task 2 Plants need certain things to

Task 2 · True or false?

- ✺ Sort these sentences into two groups, **true** and **false**.

- ✺ Write down two lists.

- ✺ Now make a list of the things you think all green plants need to stay alive and grow.

> **Plants only grow when the Sun is out. If it's a cloudy day, they don't grow.**

> **All plants have to grow in soil.**

> **Plants must have water to grow.**

> **Plants must have light to grow strong and healthy.**

> **There isn't any air on the Moon, but plants wouldn't mind. They would still grow if you gave them water and put them in the light.**

> **Plants don't mind how hot it gets, but they die if it gets too cold.**

4

Plants reproduce.

Mosses make spores inside a spore capsule.

After a while, the spore capsules split open. Thousands of tiny spores are released.

A few of the spores will land in a suitable place and new moss plants grow. All the other spores are wasted.

Fact File

Different ways of reproducing

Plants reproduce in different ways. Here are two different ways.

Someone cuts a piece from a plant. This is called a cutting.

The cutting is dipped in rooting powder. This is a powder which encourages roots to grow from the stem.

The cutting is planted and roots begin to grow. A new plant grows.

Task 3 Taking cuttings

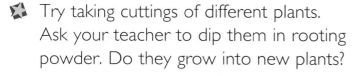

Try taking cuttings of different plants. Ask your teacher to dip them in rooting powder. Do they grow into new plants?

Ask your teacher to check that you are using the knife safely. If you want to use rooting powder, ask your teacher to dip the cuttings in the powder.

Now try this

Find out the answer to one of these questions.

- Can you grow cuttings from leaves as well as stems?
- Will the cutting grow if you don't use rooting powder?
- Do all plants grow from cuttings?

Task 4: The Canadian pondweed story

A few plants grow roots easily from a broken-off stem. They do not need to be dipped in rooting powder. Canadian pondweed is one of these.

Below there are some sentences that tell how Canadian pondweed came to Britain.

✿ Put them in an order that makes sense.

✿ Use Photocopy Master 2 to cut out and order the sentences.

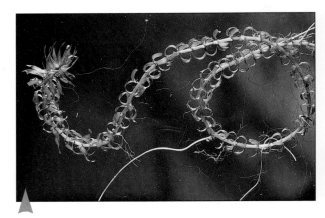

Close-up of Canadian pondweed

The hulls or bottoms of the barges broke off bits of plants as they went along. The plants fell in the mud and grew roots.

Canadian pondweed did not grow in Britain before 1847.

The timber from Canada sometimes went to Market Harborough.

People think the first bit of Canadian pondweed came across from Canada attached to a piece of timber.

Ships from Canada brought Canadian timber, or wood, to Britain.

In this way, Canadian pondweed spread along the canals and rivers.

Barges travelled along the canals and rivers.

Canadian pondweed is very common today.

Market Harborough was at the centre of Britain's canal and river system.

Within 40 years, Canadian pondweed had spread to most parts of Britain.

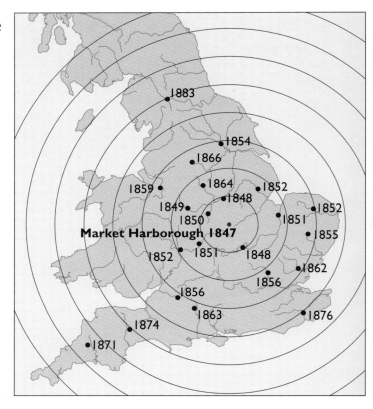

This map shows how long it took for Canadian pondweed to spread through Britain.

✿ Now sort the sentences on Photocopy Master 3 into true or false.
Use the map to help you.

Task 5

What are your ideas about seeds and fruits?

Another way that plants reproduce is by making seeds. Plants grow from these seeds. But where do seeds come from? How are they made?

This is what some children said.
Do you agree?

On the plant's stem there is a leaf part, a flower part and a seed part. They are all separate from each other.

The plant makes seeds. Parts of the flower make the seed.

There is a special leaf on the plant. It changes into a fruit or a pod. You find the seeds inside the fruit or the pod.

Seeds come from packets. You buy them from shops and garden centres. A factory makes the seeds.

✦ Use Photocopy Master 4 to draw and write to show where you think seeds come from.

✦ Use the words on the right to make a **concept map** of your ideas.

fruit

seed

pollen

plant

flower

leaf

7

Where do seeds come from?

Look at these pictures. Each line starts with a seed and goes backwards to show where it came from.
What does the last picture in each line show?

Orange tree			
The seed	. . . and before that	. . . and before that	. . . and before that.

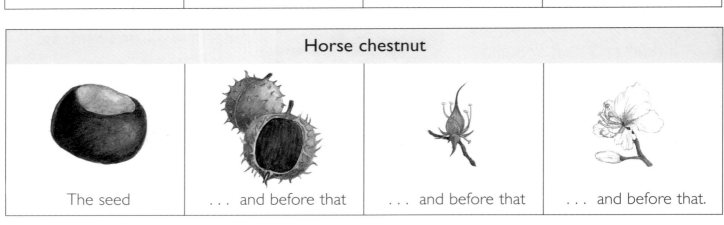

Dandelion			
The seed	. . . and before that	. . . and before that	. . . and before that.

Horse chestnut			
The seed	. . . and before that	. . . and before that	. . . and before that.

◈ Now try this

More about seeds

Draw pictures of three more seeds and the flowers they came from.
Use other books to help you.

A closer look at a flower

Flowers are an important part of the life cycle of flowering plants. A flower is made up of several different parts.

This is a cherry tree. It has pink flowers.

Each flower looks like this.

This picture shows you what you might see if the flower was cut in half. It shows you the different parts. It tells you what these parts are called.

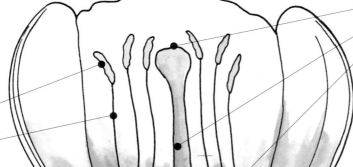

stigma
style
ovary
Together these parts make the female part of the flower. This is called the **carpel** or **pistil**.

anther
filament
Together these parts make the male part of the flower. This is called the **stamen**.

petal
The petals attract insects to the flower.

sepal
The sepals are a type of leaf. They protect the flower before it opens.

Task 8 Taking flowers apart

✦ If you take a flower apart very carefully
you can see all the different parts.
You can stick them on to card and make
a flower card.
These pictures show you how to do it. ▶

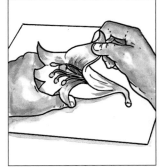

Put the flower on
white paper. Carefully
take it apart.

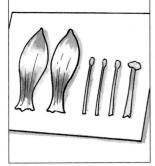

Stick the parts on to
a strip of card. Put
the glue on the card,
not the flower parts.

✦ Look at the flower cards.
Find the following things on the cards.

petal	style	sepal
filament	stamen	stigma
anther	ovary	carpel or pistil

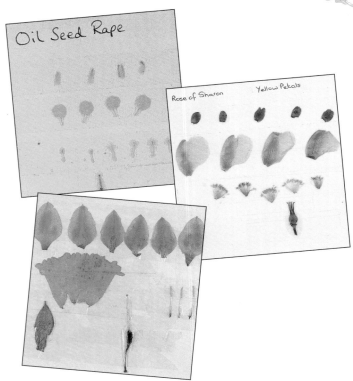

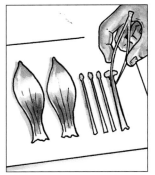

You may need to
use tweezers to
move some of the
smaller parts.

Let the glue dry.
Cover the card with
sticky-backed plastic
or sticky tape.

PCM
5

✦ Draw and label parts of flowers on
Photocopy Master 5.

Task 9 Make an identification card for your flower

✦ Suppose you had to tell your flower apart
from all the others. How could you do it?

PCM
6

✦ Record as much detail as you
can on your flower ID card.
Take measurements and draw pictures.

✦ You could use a computer to help you
make your flower ID card.

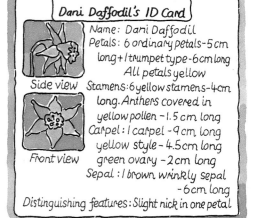

Dani Daffodil's ID Card

Name: Dani Daffodil
Petals: 6 ordinary petals-5cm
long+1 trumpet type-6cm long
All petals yellow
Side view   Stamens:6 yellow stamens-4cm
long. Anthers covered in
yellow pollen-1.5cm long
Carpel: 1 carpel-9cm long
yellow style-4.5cm long
green ovary-2cm long
Front view   Sepal: 1 brown wrinkly sepal
-6cm long
Distinguishing features: Slight nick in one petal

Fact File

Pollen looks like a fine powder. It is usually a yellowish colour. It is produced in the anther.

The stigma is usually slightly sticky on top to help it catch the pollen.

Making the seed

A flowering plant needs to make seeds that are able to grow into new plants.
To do this, pollen, from the male part of the plant, must reach the stigma.

When pollen lands on the stigma, we say the plant has been **pollinated**. A lot of plants cannot be pollinated by their own pollen.

The pollen must land on another plant of the same type. For example, the pollen from the flower of one cherry tree must go to the stigma of the flower on another cherry tree. This is called **cross-pollination**.

The pollen must travel from one plant to another. How can it do this? Sometimes the wind blows it. Sometimes insects carry the pollen. When pollen is carried by insects the plant must attract insects to the flower. They do this by making sugary stuff called nectar.

Insects feed on the nectar. These plants also often have beautifully coloured petals and sweet scents. Cherry blossom pollen is carried from one plant to another by insects.

 Task 10

The Pollen Paratroopers

Here is the start of a strip cartoon.
The Pollen Paratroopers from the Cherry Blossom Division have to reach their destination – the sticky stigma on the next tree.

 Complete the cartoon.

Fact File

Getting fertilized

When the pollen reaches the stigma, you might think that its journey was over. It isn't.

A special part of the pollen called the male cell has to travel down the inside of the female plant, right down to the ovary. When it reaches the ovary we say the plant has been **fertilized** and seeds start to form inside the ovary.

When the pollen lands on the sticky stigma, something remarkable happens. A tiny tube, called a pollen tube, grows down the style and into the middle of the ovary. The male cell goes down the tube and enters the middle of the ovary.

After this, seeds start to grow. It is usually the ovary of the flower which becomes the **fruit** containing seeds. The way we use the word 'fruit' in everyday life is rather different to the way we use the word when we are being scientific. In everyday life, we think of fruits as only those fruits which are good to eat. In science, a fruit is the part of a plant where seeds develop. They don't have to taste good!

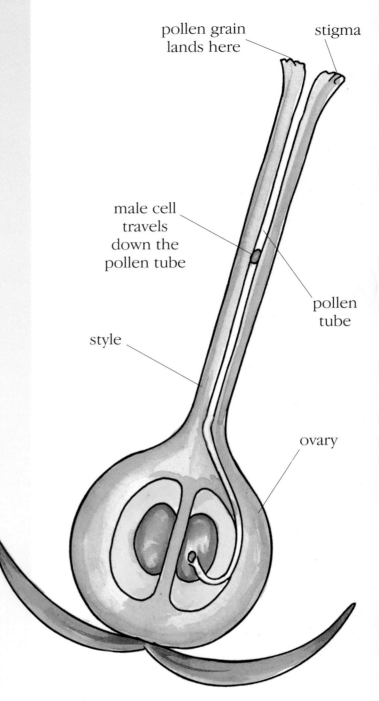

pollen grain lands here
stigma
male cell travels down the pollen tube
style
pollen tube
ovary

I must get some fruit for tea.

Mmm, there are some interesting fruit on these plants.

Everyday use

Scientific use

Fact File

Finding fruits

Fruits come in all shapes and sizes. Here are some of them.

blackberry

lupin

dandelion

wood aven

Task 11

Go on a fruit hunt

⚹ Look for fruits on all types of flowering plants. Remember, it is a part of the **flower** that will turn into the fruit. Sometimes you can spot fruits beginning to grow before the flower dies.

⚹ Choose one fruit. Carefully draw the outside.

⚹ Ask an adult to cut it in half. Find the seeds inside.

⚹ Use a magnifier. Draw a seed.

fruit

seed

⚹ Now look at another fruit.

⚹ Look closely at an orange.

⚹ Look at it with a partner.

⚹ Look at each end.

⚹ Can you see a difference between them? One end has what's left of the sepals. The other end is a small scar. It is where the stigma and style used to be.

⚹ Look back at the pictures of the orange on page 8.
Which part of the plant is the bit we eat?
Where are the seeds?

⚠ Safety note: Ask an adult to cut the orange.

◄ oranges

Fact File

British baked beans

Sometimes scientists take the pollen from one plant and transfer it to another plant. They do this so that they can grow new plants with special features. Recently, scientists have done this to make a British baked bean plant.

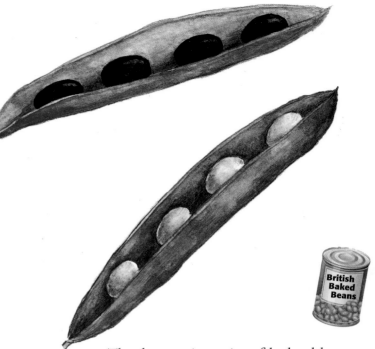

The beans in a tin of baked beans are the seeds of a bean plant. Most beans grown in cool Britain are black. The beans grown in warmer America are white. People prefer to eat white beans. They are not used to the look of black beans in tomato sauce.

Some British bean plants had a few white beans. The scientists used the pollen from these plants to pollinate and fertilize other bean plants. Only the plants which produced the most white seeds were used to grow the next lot of beans.

After 20 years, scientists were able to grow plants in Britain which made only white beans. The British baked bean had arrived. One supermarket is already selling British beans. Now we won't have to buy so many baked beans from America.

Fact File Getting away from it all

Once the seed is fully formed it is ready to make a new plant. Plants make lots of seeds but most of them will not grow into new plants. The seeds get destroyed or damaged or end up somewhere where plants can't grow.

lupin

wood aven

blackberry

The seed has a better chance of surviving if it does not land right next to the parent plant. This is because the parent plant may take the light and water that the new plant needs to grow.

ash

dandelion

When seeds travel away from their parent plant, we call it **seed dispersal**. Plants have many different ways of dispersing their seed.

Task 12 Talking seeds

Copy out the speech bubbles. Write the correct name of the plant next to each speech bubble.

A dandelion

B bramble or blackberry

C wood aven

D lupin

E ash

Use Photocopy Master 7 to show how different plants disperse their seeds.

I've got a juicy covering. Birds think it's really tasty. They eat up the fruit. I go right through the bird and come out the other end. I travel miles this way.

I'm light as a feather. The wind catches me and blows me away. I've got my own tiny parachute. It helps to keep me in the air.

I sit in a pod with lots of other seeds. When the pod is ripe it splits open and twists at the same time. All of us seeds explode out of the pod.

I hitch a ride on any passing animal. I've got hooks sticking out to catch in their fur.

I've got a wing attached to me. It makes a brilliant spinner. When the wind catches it, I go spinning away.

Fact File

Poppy population

There are four types of red poppy growing in the British Isles. In each poppy, the ovary grows into a capsule inside the petals. Thousands of seeds grow inside the capsule. Look at the photograph of the capsules. Each capsule looks as if it has a hat. Just under the hat you should be able to see small holes. It looks a bit like a pepperpot. The seeds are shaken out of the holes when the capsule sways in the wind. The seeds are dispersed by the wind.

poppy

capsules with seeds

Task 13 · More about poppies

Here is some more information about poppies. The maps show you two things: where each type of poppy grows and a rough idea of how many poppies grow there. More dots mean more poppies.

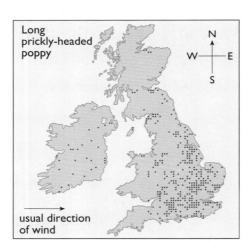
Long prickly-headed poppy
N
W — E
S
usual direction of wind

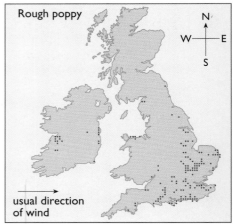
Rough poppy
N
W — E
S
usual direction of wind

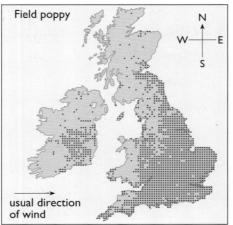
Field poppy
N
W — E
S
usual direction of wind

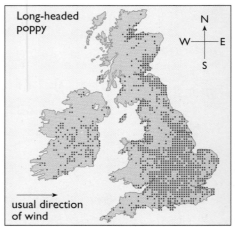
Long-headed poppy
N
W — E
S
usual direction of wind

This table gives the number of seeds each type of poppy makes.

Name of poppy	Number of seeds made from one plant
Field poppy	170 000 (or about 170 thousand)
Long-headed poppy	13 700 (or about 14 thousand)
Prickly-headed poppy	2 142 (or about 2 thousand)
Long rough-headed poppy	1 680 (or about 1½ thousand)

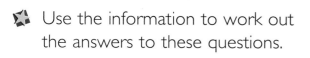

✸ Use the information to work out the answers to these questions.

✸ Write down your answers.

① Which poppy do you think is the most common poppy in England. Why?

② Which poppy do you think is the rarest poppy in Britain? Why?

③ Do more poppies grow in the west or the east of Britain? Why?

④ What do you think the maps would look like if poppies were dispersed by animals and not by the wind?

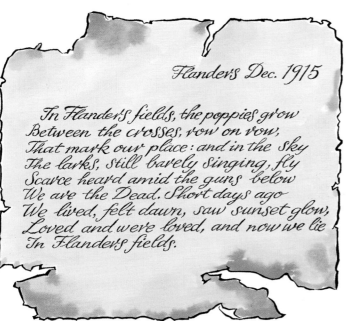

Flanders Dec. 1915

In Flanders fields, the poppies grow
Between the crosses, row on row,
That mark our place: and in the sky
The larks, still bravely singing, fly
Scarce heard amid the guns below
We are the Dead. Short days ago
We lived, felt dawn, saw sunset glow,
Loved and were loved, and now we lie
In Flanders fields.

Task 14 Poppies in poetry

This is a poem about poppies. It was written in December 1915 by a man called Colonel John McRee.

✸ Read the poem.

✸ Find out what was happening in Europe in 1915. Each year on Remembrance Day, many people wear poppies. Why do you think this is?

Fact File

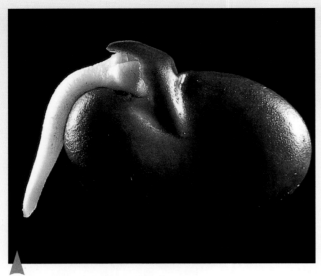

Bean seed with radicle

Germination

Beginning again

Each plant makes far more seeds than it needs. When the seeds are dispersed, most of them end up in places where they cannot grow. Only a few seeds land in the right place for them to begin to grow or **germinate**. A seed will only germinate if it has enough water and air, a suitable temperature and it is ready to grow.

You can tell when a seed starts to germinate. A small root called a **radicle** comes out of the seed. Here is a photograph of a bean seed. It has germinated. You can see its radicle.

 Put some kitchen paper around the inside of a cut-off pop bottle.

 Put scrunched-up newspaper or paper towels in the middle. Pour some water into the bottle. Make the kitchen paper damp.

Task 15 How long do different seeds take to germinate?

Here is one way to germinate seeds. It is a good idea to put in two or three seeds in case one of the seeds doesn't grow.

 Try germinating seeds from different plants.

 Find out how many days it takes for each type of seed to germinate.

 PCM 8

 Record your results in a table. Use Photocopy Master 8.

Drop seeds between the kitchen paper and the bottle.

 Watch them germinate over the next few days.

Task 16 Fast plants

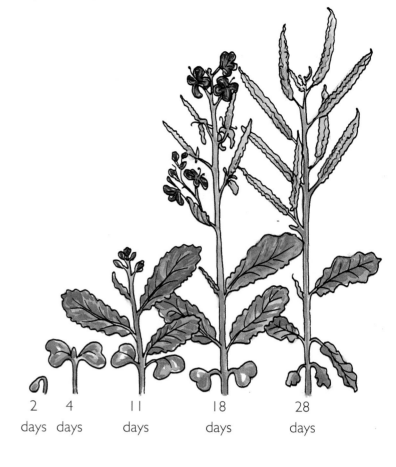

| 2 | 4 | 11 | 18 | 28 |
| days | days | days | days | days |

✖ Like all plants, flowering plants have a life cycle. Plants grow flowers. The flowers are pollinated. The fruit grows, then seeds grow in the fruit. The seeds are dispersed. Some of the seeds germinate. They grow into plants. The plants grow flowers, and so it goes on.

Most plants take quite a long time to go through their life cycle. Often it takes a whole year. The plant in the diagram is special. It takes only about six weeks to go through its life cycle. These plants are a type of **brassica**, but everyone calls them 'fast plants'. The table gives some information about the way they grow.

✖ Use the information on the table to plot a line graph of the plant's height over the first 35 days.

✖ Put all the days from 0 to 35 on the horizontal axis, so that they are evenly spaced. Show your graph on Photocopy Master 9.

✖ Write the answers to these questions. Use your graph to help you.

Time in days	Height above ground in cm
2	1
4	3
7	4
11	8
15	15
18	18
25	20
30	20
35	20

① When was the plant about 8 cm high?

② What height would you expect the plant to be on day 14?

③ Between which days did the plant grow fastest?

④ At the end, the line on your graph is flat. Why is this?

⑤ Draw a picture of what you think the plant might look like on day 15.

Task 17 Pollination Street

- Work in a group.

- Make up a play or mime about the life of a plant.

- Decide who will play the parts.

- Design a programme.

The Plant Players present Pollination Street

Act 1° The plants grow flowers

Act 2° The flowers are pollinated by a bee

Act 3° The seeds disperse on the wind. They germinate and grow into new plants

Cast List

Act 1°
Plants
Rain
Sun

Anna, Sam
Jake
Hannah

Act 2°
1st flower
2nd flower
Bee

Melanie
Lee
Dave

Act 3°
Seeds

Everyone

Glossary for Plant Reproduction

anther:
carpel (or pistil):
filament:
fertilization: This is when a special part from the pollen goes right into the ovary
fruit:
germination:
life cycle:
ovary:
pollen:
pollination:
seed:
seed dispersal:
stamen:
stigma:
style:

Task 18 Make a glossary

A glossary is a list of special words with their meanings.

PCM 10

- The picture shows the start of a glossary of words about plant reproduction. Use Photocopy Master 10 to make a glossary.

Plants can be harmed.

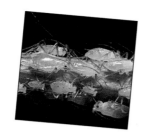

Plants are living things. They can be harmed. Humans often harm plants. Many of the things we do harm plants. Many of the things we make and use harm plants. Natural things, like other animals or extreme weather conditions, can also harm plants.

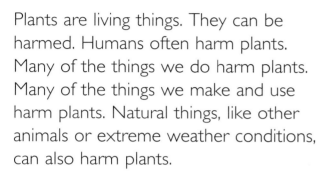

Work with a partner.
Make a list of different ways to harm plants.

Have a competition in the class.
See who can make the longest list.

Fact File

Plants and salt

We put salt on icy roads in winter. It stops the water on the road's surface freezing unless it gets very cold – much colder than we usually get in the British Isles. But how does salt affect plants? Does the amount of salt in the soil affect their growth?

you need:

- a team of Star Investigators
- salt
- some cress seeds
- water
- a teaspoon
- some beakers
- a syringe
- 5 small containers
- cotton wool

Task **19** **Salt and cress**

Plan an investigation to find out how the amount of salt affects the way that cress grows.

Put some cotton wool in five small containers such as plastic lids. Put the same amount of cress seeds in each one.

Fill in a planning board.

PLANNING BOARD

Our question _____

We will change _____

We will measure _____

We will keep
these things
the same to
make our test
fair _____

This is the table we will use. (Put in the headings. Fill in the left-hand column.)

We will use
these things _____

How much salt we put in 200 ml of water	What the cress looked like			
	after 1 day	after 2 days	after 3 days	after 4 days
None				
$\frac{1}{4}$ teaspoon				
$\frac{1}{2}$ teaspoon				
$\frac{3}{4}$ teaspoon				
1 teaspoon				

✿ Use this table as part of your planning board.

✿ You must decide how to keep the test fair. Decide how much water or salty water you will give the seeds each time you water them.
Decide how often you will water them.
What else must you keep the same?

✿ Show your plans to your teacher.

✿ Make up beakers or other containers with the different amounts of salt.
Put labels on them so you know which is which.

✿ Look at your plants each day.
Fill in the table.
Try to use some of the special words about plants that you have learnt so far such as germinate and radicle.

✿ Write down what you found out. What would you expect to happen to roadside plants when the roads are salted?

Task 20 Where have all the rainforests gone?

Work in pairs or groups to find out the answers to some of these questions.

 Use books, maps and CD-ROMs.

> If we go on cutting down rainforests at this rate, how long will they last?

> What can we do to stop it happening?

> How much rainforest do we lose each year?

> What happens to the soil when the trees are cut down?

> Where are the rainforests?

> What plants and animals live in the rainforest?

> Why do people cut down rainforests?

> Why are rainforests important?

Fact File

Animal dangers

This is a picture of small insects called aphids. They cluster on the newly-grown tender stems. They feed on the plant juices and make a sweet juice called honeydew.

Ants like drinking honeydew so they 'milk' the aphids. Whenever you see aphids in a garden, look for ants as well. You often see them together. Look at some plants to see how aphids harm them.

Too much of a good thing?

Fertilizers help plants to grow more. Farmers often use fertilizers on their crops.

This graph shows you how much maize (corn) farmers could expect to get from a small field. It shows what would happen if they used different amounts of fertilizer. Fertilizer is quite expensive. Farmers do not want to waste money.

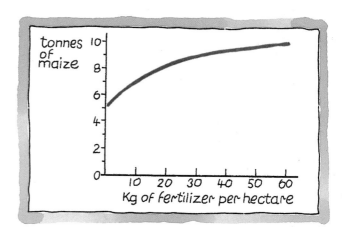

Three farmers are talking about fertilizers. They are all going to grow maize on small fields which are about the same size. The fields are about one hectare in size.

I'm going to put about 50 kg of fertilizer on my maize this year. I'll get a much better crop that way.

I think I might go for about 20 kg of fertilizer. I don't think there's any point putting more on.

I'm only going to put about 10 kg on mine. It's too expensive to put more on.

Imagine you are a farming adviser. What would you say to each farmer?

Use the graph to help you plan your answers.

Write your answers on Photocopy Master 11.

Now try this

Sometimes, too much fertilizer is put on fields. The part that isn't used by the crop gets washed into rivers and streams. This can harm plants and animals in the rivers and streams.

Write a letter to a farmer warning him about the problems that can be caused by using too much fertilizer.

Plants make their own food. This makes plants different from animals.

What goes into a plant?

The next idea you will learn about in this book is to do with plants and their food.

Where do plants come from?
What do they take in?
Where does their food come from?

 PCM 12

Make a list of the things that plants take in. Write beside each word how much you think they take in. Write '**some**' or '**a little**' or '**hardly any**' or '**lots**'.

Write your ideas about where plant food comes from.

A science story

Over the years, many people have wondered what plants are made of. After all, you don't see plants tucking into a plate of fish and chips! Many people think that plants take in a lot of soil or earth.

This is a story about a Dutch scientist called Jean-Baptiste Van Helmont. He tried to find what plants take in. He lived in Holland over 300 years ago.

Imagine that Jean-Baptiste was alive today. This is what he might say.

I wanted to find out what plants are made of. I wanted to find out how much soil went into a growing tree.
This is what I did.
I decided to plant a young willow tree in a big pot of soil. Before I did this, I weighed two things. I weighed the tree. It was 2 kg. I dried the soil, and then I weighed it. The dry soil was 90 kg. For the next five years I watered the plant. The only thing I gave it was water. It grew really well.
After five years I took out the tree. I weighed it again. Now it weighed 76 kg. I dried and weighed the soil again. It weighed 89.95 kg.

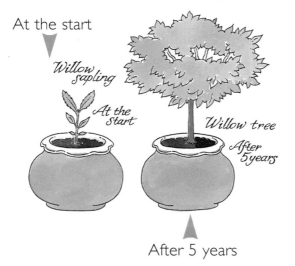

At the start
Willow sapling
At the start
Willow tree
After 5 years

After 5 years

 PCM 13

Read the story and answer the questions on Photocopy Master 13.

① Van Helmont found out that plants take in very little from the soil. This makes sense. If trees took in lots of soil there would be a hole in the ground under every tree!

② Plants are different to animals. They do not take in food in the way that we do. Plants do something completely different. This is what they do.

③ Something special happens inside the plant so that it can change the carbon dioxide and water into sugar and oxygen.

④ Plants can only make food in the light. They use the energy from the sunlight to change the carbon dioxide and the water into sugar and oxygen.

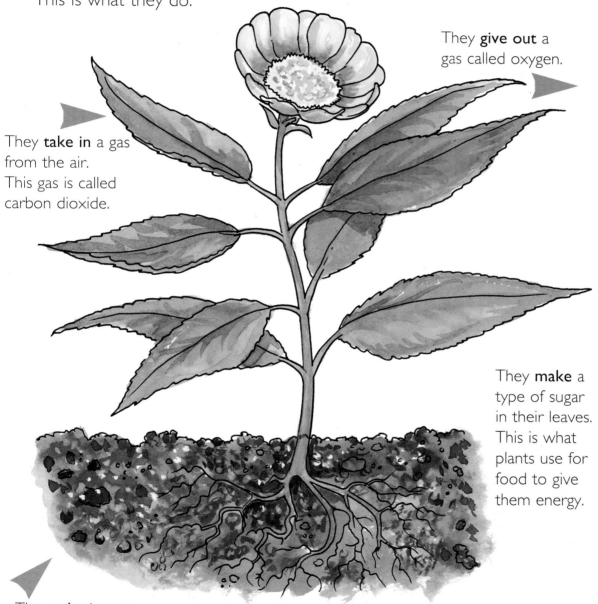

They **give out** a gas called oxygen.

They **take in** a gas from the air. This gas is called carbon dioxide.

They **make** a type of sugar in their leaves. This is what plants use for food to give them energy.

They **take in** water through their roots.

It's light. I can make food now. I can use that food to keep me going.

It's dark. I can't make food now. I will have to use the food I made in the day to keep me going.

Plants are amazing! Humans may be clever but we can't make our food from just water and carbon dioxide. Read this cartoon.

Plants make their own food. Animals do not. This is why we call plants **producers**. They produce (make) their own food.

We call animals **consumers**. This is because they take in 'ready-made' food. Animals either eat plants or they eat other animals. All food comes from plants originally. This is one reason why plants are so important to us.

Task 24 What do you take in?

🎇 Read the Fact File on the right.

🎇 Think of the food you eat in a typical day. Make a list.

🎇 Now imagine how much food you take in during your lifetime. You will probably live for about 27 000 days.

🎇 Think of a plant. Plants mainly take in just water and carbon dioxide.

PCM 14

🎇 Draw two pictures. Show what is taken in during a lifetime by you, and by a plant. Use Photocopy Master 14.

Fact File

More about what plants take in

close-up photo of a plant leaf

Plants take in different things. Some of these things get used by the plant to make food. Here is some more information about plants.

Plants take in lots of water. They only use a little bit of water to make food. They use the rest in other ways.

Plants take in air. Air is made up of lots of different gases. Carbon dioxide is one of the gases in air. There is only a small amount of carbon dioxide in the air. But this is the gas that plants use to make their food.

A lot of the material that plants are made of started out as the gas carbon dioxide.

Plants also take in minerals from the soil. They only take in tiny amounts. They help the plant stay healthy. They are not used by the plant to make the food which gives them energy to live and grow.

close-up of a plant's root

plant roots

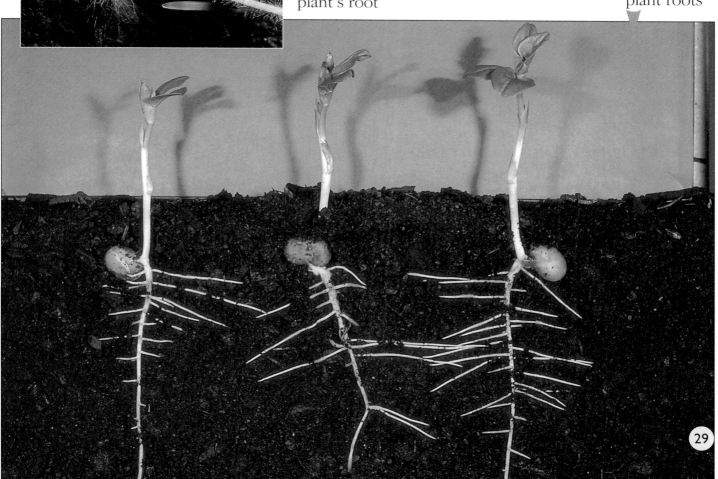

Task 25 A recipe for making plant food

When a plant makes its own food it starts off with raw materials (carbon dioxide and water) and changes them into something new (sugar and oxygen). When we bake a cake we do something similar. Below is a recipe for a cake.

✦ Design a recipe for making plant food.
What are the ingredients?
What is needed to make them change?
What is the end result?
Show all these things on your recipe.

These are the things you start with.

The heat from the oven provides energy for the change to take place.

This is what you have made.

Ingredients
Take the following things and mix them together:

flour
egg
sugar
margarine

How to make them change
Mix them up together and put them in the oven. Bake them to make them change into cake.

The end result
Take out the cooked cake.

Task 26 If only they could talk . . .

✦ Imagine that a tree and a fox could talk and that they were having a conversation about the way they get their food. The cartoon suggests how it might start.

✦ Make up a conversation between a fox and a tree. You can finish off this one or start another one of your own.

So fox, you think I've got it easy do you? Well, think again . . .

It's all right for you, tree. You just stand still. I have to chase my food.

Checkpoint

What do you know now?

 Look back to some of your ideas when you started thinking about plants.
Where did you think seeds came from?
How did you think plants got their food?
Do you think the same now?
How have your ideas changed?

 Answer the questions on this page and page 32 to help you find out what you have learnt.

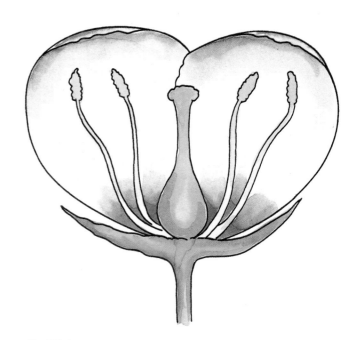

① This diagram shows half a flower. Label the different parts. Underline the male parts in red and the female parts in blue. Use Photocopy Master 15.

② Here are some photographs of different things happening to plants. Write the correct word for each set of photographs or photograph.
Use these words: **germination, pollination, seed dispersal**.
Use Photocopy Master 16.

Checkpoint
continued

③ Here are some things people might say about plants. They are all wrong. How would you put them right? Write down what you would say.

> It doesn't matter if we harm plants. They aren't important to us.

> Plants take in lots of soil. Soil is their food.

> If you put plants in the dark they will still grow. Light isn't important to them.

> I remember learning about plants at school. To make their food they take in oxygen and water.

④ Sort these living things into **producers** and **consumers**. Make two lists.

A

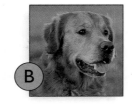
B

C

D

E

F

G

H

I